OPEN
Arms

OPEN *Arms*

CONTINUING THE ELKINS' INSPIRING
ADOPTION JOURNEY

RUSSELL ELKINS

Open Arms: Continuing the Elkins' Inspiring Adoption Journey
By Russell Elkins
©2013 Russell Elkins

Some of the names in this book have been changed to protect the privacy of
the individuals involved.

Edited by Chris White of C.P. White Media, limited company
www.cpwhitemedia.com
Beta readers and proofreaders: Jenna Lovell, Bryan Elkins, Melanie Elkins,
Kristyn Runyan, Sherley Hodes.

Cover photo and author photo by Jammie Elkins Photography
Cover design by Inky's Nest Publishing
Interior book design by Inky's Nest Publishing

Published by Inky's Nest Publishing

RussellElkins.com
1st edition
First printed in 2013 in the United States of America

To my beautiful children.
You make me always want to be a better man.

Table of Contents

Chapter 1

One Step Behind

When my big brother got in trouble for something, my parents would make me sit through a long lecture right along with him. Chances were good that I had either done it also (but without getting caught) or that I would have done it if I had the chance.

We did everything together.

Clark is only eighteen months older than me. We had the same interests, the same group of friends, and the same goals in life, so I was always just one step behind him. That was fine with me. I liked where we were going.

After I graduated from high school, I applied to the same university he was attending. While studying for my degree, two years after Clark had gotten married, I asked my girlfriend to marry me. Amber and I had been dating for about a year and a half. Everything seemed perfectly in line for us to live happily ever after.

Clark and his wife, Beth, didn't wait very long before they decided to have children. Their daughter, Evie, was born roughly a year after they were married. Amber and I weren't planning to have children as quickly as they had, but only about a month after we'd gotten married, she told me she might be pregnant. Even though we had no money and school kept us very busy, the prospect of becoming a father excited me.

About the time Amber told me she thought she could be pregnant was also when things started to crumble between us. Things had actually started to fall apart even before our marriage had gotten started, but it took me about a month of naiveté to realize just how much trouble our relationship was in. I had been waking up every morning with a bright smile, excited my new bride was next to me, while she was struggling to find happiness in life.

As a result, when she told me that she thought she might be pregnant—and I was bouncing off the walls with excitement—the chasm between our levels of optimism broadened even more.

It turned out Amber wasn't pregnant, so my dream of being a father would have to wait.

Soon after that happened she told me that she was sorry, but she didn't think she loved me like a wife should love her husband. She wondered out loud if she had made a big mistake in getting married.

We were able to keep it together for a few more weeks, but things were very different than they were before. She struggled to explain it to me because she couldn't find the words and she didn't think I could understand. In the end she decided that she needed some time and space to figure things out.

After being married less than two months, I came home from work to find her packing up the little blue Mazda Protégé. With tears in her eyes, she said she was sorry. She hugged me goodbye, and I watched her drive away.

I was all alone.

She didn't know when or if she would be coming back.

The road I had been traveling on—the one that I thought would keep me a step behind my big brother—was no longer leading me where I wanted to go. Amber and I talked every day on the phone, but she wouldn't say she loved me, and I couldn't get her to come back. Months later, when my birthday was approaching, I asked for just one thing: permission to come see her. When she shot that idea down and gave me a gift certificate instead, I knew it was time to start considering some difficult decisions. A little more time passed. Any hope I had left for us was gone, and I knew it was over. Our divorce was finalized less than a week after filing the paperwork.

Not only was the girl who I had expected to be my eternal companion gone, but the other person who I felt closest to, my big brother, had just moved to Philadelphia for dental school. As soon as I could spare time away from my classes I hopped on a plane and flew out to Pennsylvania in the hope of escaping the reality of my life for a while.

My flight arrived too late in the evening to catch my niece Evie before her bedtime, but I just had to see her. As Clark and I stood over her toddler bed watching her sleep, I said, "You're the luckiest guy in the world." Clark was a poor dental school student without a penny to his name, but in my eyes he was rich. He had everything.

I threw an air mattress onto Evie's bedroom floor and shut my eyes for the night. In the morning, as the sun began to peek through the blinds, I watched her as she started to stir herself awake. Her eyes widened when she saw me and an enormous grin spread across her face. When I had last seen her she couldn't even walk, but she ran across the room and jumped into my arms. We sat there for a long time just holding each other. Playing the role of uncle wasn't quite the same as playing the role of father, but I was very grateful to have what I did have.

Months later, when a new semester started, Amber came back to town. Out of 30,000 students attending the university, she seemed to be the only person I bumped into on a regular basis. Conversations were short and cordial at first, but after running into each other so often, our conversations became deeper. On a few different occasions we talked late into the night about all the things that had happened over the last year. She was able to open up and share some things she had kept inside while we were married. I still didn't agree with her choice to leave, but I was finally getting a clearer understanding about why she *had*. Spending time together in intimate conversation brought back a lot of the feelings we used to share.

I had been spending months trying to reject the feelings I still had for Amber, but having her near me again brought them rushing back. And although I had my family to fall on for support through the divorce, I couldn't talk to them about what was going on inside me for fear that they'd smack me upside the head and tell me I was crazy for even being around her.

I didn't know what to do.

I didn't know what I wanted.

Plus, I had to figure it all out on my own.

Then one night after one of our long and intimate conversations, I lay on my bed thinking about everything. My mind went in circles for the first few hours, but around four o'clock in the morning I began to see things clearly for the first time in a long time. I lay there the entire night deep in my emotions, deep in thought. When the time came for me to get up and go to class, even though I hadn't caught a minute of sleep, I got up and went about my day.

It was a very difficult decision to make, but I knew what I wanted. I knew where I wanted to go. It was time to start over completely. Although I continued to bump into Amber everywhere I went on campus, I was finally able to let her go and start closing that chapter of my life for good.

It took me some time before I was even remotely interested in dating again. After a few interesting relationships, one Sunday in church I noticed a beautiful blonde I'd never seen before. Jammie and I hit it off from the first time I cornered her by the drinking fountain and asked her name. She was exactly who I was looking for, and before long I found myself standing nervously in front of her father, asking for his blessing to marry her.

Jammie and I first decided that we wanted to become parents about six months after we were married, but we didn't put forth much effort to make it happen. The only thing we did was decide not to renew her birth control prescription. For a lot of our friends that was all that was needed.

Years went by and we gradually put forth more and more effort. We began to try anything that might help our chances of getting pregnant (even some silly remedies that were based more on superstition than science). I had graduated from college and begun my career. We had found a new life in Idaho. We'd made new friends. Everything in our life was progressing except for our goal to become parents.

For financial reasons, as well as our pride, we had been resisting the idea of seeing a fertility specialist. After so many years of failing to have children, though, we had tried everything else. It was time. We tried a variety of treatments, but never saw any positive results.

After about four and a half years of wishing we were parents and not much else, we began to change our way of thinking. There were still quite a few fertility treatments we hadn't tried, but we had grown weary of trying to build our family that way. We wanted out of the emotional cycle that was forcing us to begin each month hoping our new treatment would work, but which always ended with a negative pregnancy test.

It was disheartening and frustrating to want our own children so badly, and yet to feel so utterly helpless at making that dream reality.

Adoption had been poking at us in the backs of our minds for a long time, even before we had started to see a fertility specialist. Even though we had been thinking about it, we didn't want to take that step until we felt like we were ready for it. As we grew increasingly more frustrated with fertility treatments, we began to fully embrace the possibility of adoption.

We found ourselves smiling when we talked about adoption and gritting our teeth when we discussed more fertility treatments. The idea of adopting was comforting.

It just felt right.

We didn't feel like we were being forced to resort to adoption, and that was important to us. We felt like we were making the decision because it was something that we truly wanted. Having children biologically wasn't as important to us anymore. We were excited about adoption!

Like many people, Jammie and I had quite a few misconceptions about adoption when we first stepped into the adoption agency. Adoption has been around as long as humans have, but just as societies have changed over time, adoption has too.

The twentieth century saw a gradual increase in unwed pregnancies. During the earlier decades of the century people had a tendency to want to keep these things hidden from the public. In the hope of protecting privacy and anonymity, laws were enacted in the United States that sealed up adoption records, making them inaccessible to people outside the agency. This increase in privacy led to higher numbers in adoption, and as the number of unwed pregnancies continued to increase, so did the number of adoptions, peaking in 1970.

Abortion was soon legalized, and birth control became much more common, leading to a decrease in children being born to unwed parents. The 1970's also saw a sharp rise in government assistance programs for single, young, and lower income families. Society began to be more accepting of single parenthood. These things, along with other factors, contributed to a dramatic decline in the number of adoptions. In 1970 close to 9% of children born to unwed mothers were placed for adoption. By 1981 that number dropped to about 4%. Since the early 1990's, that number has not risen above 1%.

During the same period of time that the rate of adoption declined, the number of couples wanting to adopt increased. The line of people hoping to adopt grew longer and longer.

Also during this time of change, while the number of adoptions was changing, society began to change the way it viewed adoption. The desire for secrecy in adoption was being pushed aside by the increased interest of adopted children who had grown older and now wanted to reconnect with their biological families. The laws regarding adoption records began to change, and the requirement for keeping adoption records private was removed.

An increase in adopted children and biological parents wanting to reconnect led to more change in the thinking that surrounded adoption. People placing children for adoption began to expect that they would be able to keep at least some kind of connection with their biological child from the very beginning of the adoption process. These adoptions are now known as "open adoptions."

The term open adoption means that there is contact between the biological parents and the adoptive family. The amount and type of contact between those involved varies from situation to situation and state to state.

In the late 1980's, it was estimated that only about 30% of the adoption agencies in the United States even offered the possibility of open adoption. By the mid 1990's, however, that number rose to almost 75%. The agencies that didn't offer open adoption struggled to catch the interest of birth parents.

Adoption continued to evolve until open adoption wasn't just commonplace, it had become the new norm.

Jammie and I knew from the moment we began learning about open adoption that it was right for our family. We felt nervous and vulnerable when contemplating the possibilities of living with such open relationships, but we also felt strongly that it would be best for everyone involved—especially our children.

We expected to grow as individuals throughout the process. Parenthood, whether brought on by adoption or not, can do that. What we didn't fully expect was that we would learn entirely new ways to love. We didn't fully understand what it would be like to have these special relationships because they're unique to open adoption. And although the hardships in my past have helped shape me into the man that I am, I didn't anticipate how big and how direct the influence of my history would be on our adoptions.

The tools God blessed me with through my experiences with Amber prepared me for the adoption journey Jammie and I would face together.

Chapter 2

Our First Time Through

When Jammie and I first poked our heads into the adoption agency we didn't really know what we were getting ourselves into. That was when we first learned about open adoption, which appealed to us from the very beginning. Although we liked the thought of open adoption, we were unsure about just how open we wanted that relationship to be. Many of our questions couldn't be answered until we were chosen to adopt and we could begin building that relationship.

Brianna was five months pregnant and just fifteen years old when she first contacted us. We were lucky. We had only been waiting for four months, which was pretty quick for the agency we were working with.

The situation proved to be pretty complicated, though. Even though Brianna had been giving a lot of thought to the idea, and she wholeheartedly wanted to choose adoption, the birth father wasn't so eager. He didn't want to raise the baby himself, mind you, but instead wanted her to drop out of high school so *she* could do it. As a result, the hope that Jammie and I had so quickly found was just as quickly lost within the fragile nuances of our situation.

The most unique part of our story is what happened next.

Brianna decided to come to Idaho to have her baby. She chose to do this because Idaho's adoption laws, where we lived, are different than those of Mississippi, where she lived. Here in Idaho, if the birth father didn't want to raise the child, he couldn't stop her from placing the baby for adoption. In order for the adoption to proceed under Idaho state law, Brianna had to give birth here, not in Mississippi.

Hoping to avoid traveling during the last few months of her pregnancy, she jumped on a plane two months before her due date. Since there were so many things left to accomplish before our little boy was to make his debut into this world, and because we felt responsible for taking care of Brianna while she was so far away from her parents, she stayed with us in our home during those months.

Having Brianna in our home really helped us get to know our son's birth mother more intimately than most adoptive couples have the opportunity to do. That blessing went both ways—she really got to know us too. We didn't just get to know her personality; we grew to love her like family.

Brianna was a real trooper. Very few fifteen-year olds have to face something as intense as what Brianna went through, but she handled herself very maturely, especially considering that her body was swimming with pregnancy hormones and she had no local friends or family. She was amazing.

On a frigid winter day, our little boy, Ira, took his first breath. The experience brought a flood of emotions for all of us during the 48 hours we were within the hospital walls. Brianna, and her mother—who had flown out for the delivery—stayed in one hospital room while Jammie, Ira, and I stayed in another. It was surreal. I couldn't believe we were so lucky to have become connected to someone as wonderful as Brianna, and to have such a beautiful little boy to call our own.

As time drew near for us to check out of the hospital, we grew increasingly more worried. With every minute that passed we were more and more attached to Ira, but until the adoption was finalized we had no legal rights as parents. The only thing we could do was to keep caring for him, growing more and more attached.

After we left the hospital, Brianna and her mother went to stay with some of our friends a few blocks away. Her first night away from Ira was rough on her. When they came to visit the following day, as Brianna held Ira close she repeatedly whispered to him that she didn't know if she could let him go.

Brianna hurt. Even though she had already made up her mind to go through with the adoption, the act of actually doing so was very painful. Seeing her hurt so much made our hearts ache for her. While welcoming a child into our home was one of the most wonderful things we ever experienced, we felt guilty being on the receiving end of what was causing her so much pain, especially since we had grown to love her so much.

Brianna stayed in Idaho for a few more weeks to sign some custody papers with a judge, and to physically heal enough to be comfortable while traveling home.

Having little Ira in our arms was a life-changing experience. Our world began to revolve around this new little baby. The legal issues were not yet settled, though. We had Ira in our home, but custody still belonged to the adoption agency until a few months later when everything could be finalized.

Months after Brianna had gone home, Daren, the birth father, surprised all of us by serving Brianna with a subpoena. He was petitioning for custody.

We were shocked.

The things we knew about Daren, while limited, were not flattering. He was verbally abusive to her, which we had seen firsthand in the text messages he had sent to her while she'd lived with us. He had been in trouble with the law and with drugs.

Even though Brianna had already had discussions with Daren about adoption, our caseworker had advised us to get some of those conversations in writing to cover our bases. Before Ira's birth, Brianna had sent Daren a certified letter to tell him what she was doing, along with a few other text message conversations, keeping hard copies of each. At the time that our caseworker had told Brianna to do these things, we didn't think a whole lot of it. We did it as a precautionary measure, but since Daren had never shown any interest in the child, we didn't expect that to change. We felt like we had given him plenty of opportunities to take custody or take part, but he had always turned away. Those letters and text message conversations had been presented to the Idaho judge months before—when Brianna signed the custody papers— to show that he had no interest. Both Brianna's and Daren's rights had been terminated long before he began to cause a stir.

We later found out the reason for the court papers. Daren wasn't the driving force behind the sudden change. We had assumed all along that his parents knew that he'd fathered a child, but that wasn't the case. He had kept it a secret, and when his mom found out a few months after Ira was born, she decided she wanted to raise him.

The subpoena really shook us up, but it didn't amount to much. An attorney with our adoption agency delivered a letter to the judge before court, detailing everything that had occurred, and the case was immediately dismissed. With these legal issues resolved, though, we found ourselves with some ethical questions. If the biological father wanted custody of his son, could we rightfully keep him from that? In our minds, it came down to being a battle between what Brianna wanted and what Daren wanted.

Brianna wanted us to raise Ira.

Daren wanted his mother to do so.

To us, the bottom line was that Brianna's and Daren's opinions were the only ones that really mattered. At the time those decisions were being made, Brianna was the only one that showed any interest or effort in making such a tough decision. The ethical implications of the situation produced a lot of turmoil inside of me, but I felt peace about the outcome, and not just because Ira was in our home.

Although we resisted his efforts for custody, we contacted Daren three times to ask him if he wanted photographs and updates about Ira. He ignored us each time.

Over the next year, we kept steady contact with Brianna. She was able to gradually distance herself from the adoption and move on with her life. When I say she was able to move on, I don't mean she cut off contact or stopped loving Ira. We continued regular contact through letters, pictures, telephone calls, etc. As time went on, even though we had regular contact, the distance between

Idaho and Mississippi began to grow appreciably. So when Brianna and her sister bought plane tickets to come visit, we were pretty nervous.

Even though we spent nearly three months together before and after Ira's birth, being in each other's company a year later made us uncomfortable again. We didn't know how she would react to seeing Ira or even how she would react to being with Jammie and me again. We wondered if we would feel less like parents with her around.

Our worries were quickly squashed. Brianna went out of her way to make sure we knew she approved of the way we were parenting. She purposefully referred to us as Mom and Dad with Ira, helping make sure we knew she wasn't going to try to take anything away from us. Knowing she supported us the way she did made us appreciate her even more, and our bond grew much tighter while she was with us again.

Our adoption of Ira was the best thing that could have happened to us. We originally thought we would become parents the way the majority of our friends have—biologically. Adoption has never felt like a plan B for us, though. It has always felt like the plan that was meant to be.

Chapter 3

Ready to Go

Our agency's policy required us to wait one year after our adoption before we could apply to adopt again. Not long after our little boy, Ira, had finished blowing out that single candle on his birthday cake, we started discussing the possibility of adopting a second time.

We hadn't been questioning whether or not we wanted to adopt a second time, but we did have to ask ourselves how long it would take before we felt ready to do it again. Our first adoption was exhausting. Since it's an open adoption, it has an ongoing nature to it, and although the intensity of the situation ebbed over time, we felt like we were running an endurance race.

Our relationship with Brianna was going well, but it was still evolving. Change in relationships produces stress.

Ever since the very beginning of our adoption journey, we have had a tendency to obsess about it. Some days it was all we could think or talk about. It was exhausting to perpetually focus on the same thing, even if the end result was something as wonderful as the idea that we could be parents. We felt consumed by the aftermath of Ira's adoption. The inherent complexity of open adoption made our decision to adopt again more difficult than simply deciding whether or not we were ready to have a second child.

I would be lying if I didn't say we were worried about how a new open adoption relationship would go. We were fully aware that we didn't know everything about open adoption relationships just because we had done it once before. Even if we had done it ten times, every situation would be different. Yes, we felt like we were on the right path and we were succeeding with our first open adoption relationship, but the birth parents in a second adoption would be completely new; the relationships would be different. A lot of the knowledge we'd gained from our first experience would carry over to our second adoption, but not all of it.

We came to realize over time just how true that would be.

Open adoption is a good test of faith for everyone involved. Not only were we looking to add an entire birth family to our already unique family tree, but any future birth family would be taking a leap of faith with us as well, adding us to their family tree. Trust and faith would be required to make our situation work— from both sides. We had to let go of our insecurities and have confidence that God would guide all of us on our path.

Jammie and I discussed our situation, and our decision to adopt a second time came about pretty quickly. One of the biggest influences on that decision was our own experience growing up. The children in both of our families were close together in age, and having grown up that way we felt strongly that we wanted the same thing for our own children. Just how close together our children would be was largely out of our hands, since we would have to wait for birth parents to choose us, which pushed us even more to get the ball rolling as soon as possible.

We had a great experience with our adoption agency the first time, so we didn't even consider picking a new one. Also, we had already developed a great relationship with Jon, our caseworker from our first adoption, and we were excited to see that he was going to be with us on our second journey as well.

It's funny, in retrospect, how quickly we got through our paperwork. Realistically, we knew it could take a long time—maybe even years—before we were chosen to adopt again. Still, we wanted the paperwork finished as quickly as possible in case there was someone out there ready to choose us. We didn't want laziness or procrastination on our part to be the reason we missed an opportunity to be chosen.

The paperwork was incredibly tedious, just like it had been the first time, but we spent every free minute working on it until it was done. I did as much as I could, but Jammie did a lot more while I was at work than I could in my spare moments. Along with all the paperwork, we had to visit a doctor for our physicals, get background checks, do some interviews with people from the adoption agency, and have our home inspected for our home study. Even though we knew what Jon would be looking for with the home study, we still went overboard cleaning every inch of the house spotless, stressing about every tiny thing.

After the mounds of paperwork were done, it was time to choose a profile picture. The profile picture would be the first thing any potential birth parent would see, so we knew how important it was to make that first impression a good one. We chose to use a picture of us out in the snow. Jammie, being a photographer, is amazing at photo editing, so she turned our picture into a puzzle.

She removed a few of the pieces to reveal a yellow background, which was done to catch the eye of anyone browsing the pictures. We wrote a caption saying, "Are you the next piece to our family's puzzle?" We laughed about the cheesiness of the caption, but cheesy also served us well with our first profile when we caught Brianna's eye, so we weren't about to stray from our formula.

After creating the right picture, it was time to write our profile letter. We were able to reuse the majority of the profile letter from our first adoption profile. We did have to alter some sections because we were now a family of three. Plus, Jammie was now a stay-at-home mother instead of having to work a full time job like before.

After finishing our online profile, everything was turned in.

We were ready to go!

And by ready to go, I mean that we were ready to wait and wait and wait until someone chose us.

We stepped into line with about 950 other couples hoping to adopt through the same agency. There were about eighty couples waiting in Idaho alone, and the amount of adoptions that took place every year with our agency was only a fraction of that. We prepared ourselves to wait for a long time.

Even with our paperwork finished and our profile available online, we still had to finish at least ten hours of education time. We didn't stress about those hours too much since we were looking forward to an adoption conference four months away. We figured we would complete our credit hours there. That was what we had done the previous time, and we loved it.

Although the conference would give us more than enough credit hours, we were interested in a few local classes being offered, so we attended them for our own enjoyment and benefit.

In the first local class we went to, I recognized some familiar faces. I made an embarrassing mistake. I asked someone I knew from before if they were back to adopt again. I then realized I had put my foot in my mouth when he hung his head and explained how they were still waiting to adopt for the first time. And they'd been waiting since before we began the process our first time around.

Before the class officially began, the facilitator had us all introduce ourselves, and give some background about our choice to adopt. There were a few people in the class who hadn't been waiting long, and even a few who had already been chosen and were waiting for their child to be born, but a large portion of the class had been waiting for years. One couple in the room, who seemed like amazing people, had been waiting for seven years.

By the time it was our turn to introduce ourselves, we felt a little sheepish. There we were surrounded by couples who had been waiting since before we'd even thought about adopting the first time, and we were back for a second time. We told everyone that we had adopted once already and that we'd completed our paperwork as soon as we were allowed to because we expected it to take years. Nobody said or did anything to make us feel uncomfortable, but we felt guilty just knowing that so many of them had to wait so long.

The process of being chosen to adopt used to run very differently. In the days before open adoption was common, adoption agencies and caseworkers were in charge of choosing where a child would go. They placed with whomever they thought best, which often meant they placed with those who had been waiting the longest.

Now it's mostly the birth parents that choose.

Even though I could see the frustration in those who had been waiting for so long, I'm glad the system has changed. It's hard for me to imagine how it would be to have a third party try to match us with birth parents. Brianna chose Jammie and me because she saw something in us that brought her comfort. In choosing us, and choosing to have an open adoption, our lives became intertwined. Jammie and I are not perfect people, but we were a perfect match for Brianna. Her decision to choose us helped build the foundation of love that we were able to build on throughout the years to come.

The bond that began when we were first contacted was exactly what we were hoping and praying for again. We knew things would be different, and we would do our best to embrace whatever those differences would be. All we could do was continue with our faith in the process and in God.

That... and wait.

Chapter 4

The Waiting Game

An interesting thing happened right after our profile went live online. Jammie missed her period. It wasn't unusual for it to be a few days later than expected, but after being ten days late we started to wonder.

It sparked some emotions I didn't expect. I had already accepted the possibility that we might never have children biologically. Things got easier for me after accepting that. Especially after we adopted Ira, I had already let go of the need for my children to have the same genes as me.

At first my mind resisted the possibility that we were pregnant. Jammie's missed period didn't immediately fill me with hope, but just made me start to wonder. I felt like we were getting pulled into the infertility cycle all over again, which had never amounted to anything more than smashing our hopes again and again. It had happened so many times before that I didn't want to deal with it anymore.

We hadn't stressed about our infertility challenges since before Ira was born. We had already stopped listening to others' silly remedies, including the innumerable people who told us we would get pregnant as soon as we started the adoption process. All of those frustrating parts of infertility had been pushed into our past and we were focusing on adoption.

What I wanted was simple: to be a father again. The thought of having children the "normal" way was getting in the way of my goal.

I know that doesn't make sense, but in my subconscious mind the "normal" way just doesn't work for us. Any thought of trying to go about it that way would only end in more frustration. Not only that, but I was excited about adopting again. And if we were suddenly able to have biological kids, that would mean we weren't going to be adopting at the same time. I felt like we had to choose.

Those tortured feelings weren't long-lived.

My rational mind and my emotions had a little boxing match for a couple of days until my emotions finally won. I became excited about a little one running around the house, sharing my DNA, and calling me Dad.

But that wasn't the way things worked out.

Jammie and I burned through some home pregnancy tests, which all came up negative. We then tried again because the first test sticks were out of date. We tested yet again because we assumed we were testing at the wrong time of day. We tested yet again because we wondered if we were using the wrong brand. We tested and tested until her period came.

I had become excited about the possibility of my wife carrying our own baby, but when those hopes were dashed, it produced frustration. I had to flip my mental switch back to being excited about adoption. It took a day or so to return to the adoption frame of mind, but it wasn't tough.

Don't get me wrong, we never saw adoption as a last resort. Adoption was a choice for us. It was something that was already a part of our lives and we were excited about doing it again—not because we felt it was what we had to do—but because we wanted to.

It was definitely different sitting on the waiting list to adopt the second time. When we had gone through the process the first time, all we really had in our life were our dogs and an empty bedroom next to ours. This time we had little Ira sleeping in the next room, and that one little awesome fact made all the difference in the world. We didn't know if we would be contacted within a month or if it would take a decade to be selected, but at least we had our little boy to sugar coat the anxiety of the waiting game.

The answer to our question about whether it would take a month or a decade came when Jammie and I were casually lounging around the house on a lazy Sunday afternoon. Jammie's cell phone chimed, alerting her that she had just received an email. When she told me that we had just been contacted by a potential birth mother, I thought for sure she was teasing me.

This is what her email said:

Dear Russ and Jammie,
My name is Sara. I have been working with the adoption agency over the past few months searching for a family for my baby. It has been a long, hard process of trying to find a couple that I feel would be best for my child. Since we have not been introduced, I am not sure where to start or what to say.

But I'll tell you my story so that you can get to know me a little better.

I grew up in Idaho. For the past three years I have been in college, where I met my husband. Our marriage lasted five and a half months, and then we separated. A week after moving out, I discovered I was pregnant.

Despite everything that was going on, I was overjoyed to find that I would soon be a mother. However, after only a few weeks I knew I couldn't parent alone and I went back to my husband.

We worked through several months of counseling together, but it didn't work out and we finalized our divorce a few months ago. He has agreed to surrender his parental rights upon placement for adoption.

I have moved back home with my mother and will stay with her until the baby is born, and until I can fully recover from my divorce.

I have battled the idea of adoption since I got pregnant and it has taken a lot of faith to follow through and do what I know I must. About a month ago I met a potential adoptive couple, and was surprised by how much I liked them. I wanted to continue working with them but I was recently informed by the wife that they have some issues they need to resolve before they adopt a baby.

I am grateful to them though, because it opened my heart to the possibility that I could feel safe enough to trust someone else to give my baby the life she deserves—the life I cannot give her at this moment.

God has been there for me through this experience and I am relying on Him as best I can with this decision.

The second couple I chose wanted to pursue a closed adoption. We were trying to negotiate with them the kind of relationship I could have, both with them and the child, after placement. I have learned, through trying to mentally prepare myself for that kind of restricted contact, that I need an open adoption.

I know that this baby will no longer be my own, but I can in no way forget or immediately move away from this tiny spirit who has been a part of me since before she was conceived. I want to get pictures and share experiences with her parents as she grows. I want to be able to visit and be a friend to her future mother as well as a support. I want to be a part of her life in whatever small way I can.

What I would like for my baby is a home that is filled with love and laugher, to have a loving mother and father who are patient and have a stable relationship, so she will be able to look to them as an example of how a marriage should work. I want her to be taught at a young age how much God loves her so that she will never question it as she grows, as trials come. I want her to learn that she can rely on Him in all things. I want her to have the freedom to choose her likes and dislikes and be herself even if it is a little out of the ordinary for a girl, even if it's restoring old cars or something crazy. I want her to have a father who knows how to prioritize his family over other activities, to have a mother who is kind and willing to be a friend no matter how disappointed she may be in her daughter's choices.

I want her to be loved.

I felt a very strong impression when I looked through your profile that I needed to speak with you. Since I have not met you, I cannot know for sure if you are the right family for my daughter, but I would like to get to know you better. Feel free to email a response to me if you feel that my baby might belong in your family.

Sara

It had only been about a month since our profile went live online. We had already been contacted. All those couples who had been waiting for years and years were still waiting, and we possibly had a *second* child coming our way, and only within *two years* of putting our papers in the first time!

We read the letter over and over and over again.

Before we wrote her back, though, we had to tell someone. We called my brother, Clark, and then drove over to his place a few minutes away. We were bouncing off the walls with a million different emotions. We had again begun our ride on the intense emotional roller coaster that ebbed and flowed with alternating hope and caution. We couldn't help but be elated about being contacted, but at the same time we knew it could fall through at any moment.

Though we told Clark and Beth, we decided we would keep the news a secret for a while. That was a decision we had made long before, because of how things went with our first adoption. We knew we would feel secure one day and hopeless the next. It had been fun to tell people the first time, especially when the news was good, but it wasn't fun when news took a turn for the worse. We decided to keep it a secret until we knew it was a sure thing.

Jammie and I responded to Sara that same day by writing separate letters and then sending them off together. We thought it would be fun for her to get to know both of us individually as well as to see that we were both involved in the adoption process.

Since Sara had mentioned her recent divorce, I wanted to tell her about mine. I remembered very clearly all the insecurities I'd felt surrounding it—feeling judged by others, feeling like I had failed at something important, and so on. I wanted her to know I had been there. Jammie and I talked about it, though, and decided to save that conversation for another time.

We emailed our letters and then began to chew our fingernails as we waited for a response, but it didn't come that day. It didn't come the next day either, which made us twice as anxious as the previous day. When Tuesday came around, our anxiety level had reached its peak.

Then our phone rang. It was Sara's caseworker. Sara wanted to meet us face-to-face that same day.

Chapter 5

Face-to-Face

We showed up early to our appointment to meet Sara at the adoption agency. We sat nervously in the office, watching every car pull into the parking lot, wondering if Sara was driving each and every one of them. We knew her instantly when we saw her walking through the parking lot. To be fair that wasn't terribly difficult to do, since her protruding belly gave her away.

Sara thought it would be uncomfortable to have the caseworker sit in on our conversation, so she asked to be left alone with us. As we sat down with her, we didn't know if we would be chatting for ten minutes or ten hours. We also didn't know what we were going to talk about, other than the obvious. We decided to just be ourselves, and as a result conversation came easily and naturally.

We talked about what she had been going through with her decision to choose adoption—a conversation that included quite a bit about her divorce. We also discussed our first adoption and our relationship with Ira's birth mom.

Sara had been through a lot over the last year. She grew attached to the first couple she had chosen to adopt her baby, but they decided they weren't yet ready to adopt.

She started to communicate with the second couple without promising to choose them. She didn't commit completely to them because she wasn't 100% sure she was going to choose adoption, and she wasn't positive their philosophies of adoption would match with her own. When she did make a final decision regarding the second couple, she told them she would need to choose someone who also wanted an open adoption.

It broke our hearts to hear that the couple had laid a guilt trip on Sara's shoulders when she broke the news to them. The only other person besides Sara who had any say in what was going on was Caleb, her ex-husband. This baby was still their baby. Nobody else had any right to lay claim to this child: not that couple, not us, not even Caleb or Sara's extended family.

Adoptive couples should never feel entitled to someone else's child, and they should never put extra pressure on the birth parents, no matter how badly they want to become parents in their own right.

We listened to the hurt in her voice as she recounted her experience. It brought up some interesting questions and emotions.

At what point does that baby completely and solidly belong to the adoptive couple? Obviously, the simple act of being contacted by a birth mother doesn't entitle the hopeful adoptive couple. Equally as obvious was the fact that, with more than a year gone by since our son's adoption had been finalized, I would fight tooth and nail against anybody who thought about taking our son away from us.

Since I became active in the adoption community, I have seen adoptions go through a gray area in which hopeful adoptive parents feel like the child is already theirs, but legally that's not quite the case.

We had found ourselves in that gray area during our first adoption, when Brianna was pushing for the adoption to go through and Daren came out of nowhere to fight it. Our journey down the road with Caleb and Sara would indeed be very different from our first adoption, but we would nevertheless come to find ourselves yet again in that gray area where it was difficult to know where our legal and ethical rights began and ended.

We made it our main focus to assure Sara that we would support whatever decision she made. Whether or not she chose us, or even if she chose to place her child for adoption, was not for us to decide or push on her. A pressured relationship would only cause problems anyway.

Getting to know Sara was a different experience than getting to know Brianna. Brianna lived on the other side of the country, so email and Facebook were our main forms of communication. We were in contact quite a bit, but the internet is impersonal when compared to a face-to-face meeting.

Even though we had just met Sara, we were able to get deep into conversation with her. We talked heart-to-heart and shared some tears together. And even though a big part of me wanted to bring up my divorce—and assure her we weren't among those who would judge her—the window for me to do so never opened. I know that probably sounds weird since we'd talked extensively about her divorce, but it just didn't happen at this meeting. The caseworker stuck her head into the room after two hours and informed us it was time for her to start locking up the building.

The only people left in the building besides Sara's caseworker were the birth mothers (and expecting mothers considering adoption) who were attending their weekly support group down the hall. Once a week the people in the support group would come together and discuss what they were going through. Jammie used to attend the group with Brianna before Ira was born, so she had gotten to know many of the birth mothers, as well as the group leader, Virginia.

It was fun to be funneled out into the hallway all at the same time. Sara had already met with the group before, so it was nice to get a chance to chat together. When Virginia learned about why we three were meeting together, she turned to Sara and told her how awesome she thought we were.

We weren't seeking any endorsements, but to receive one from a person we all admired certainly wasn't going to hurt.

Our meeting with Sara gave us plenty to think about.

For starters, we knew a little bit more about what we were getting into this time. We knew a little bit more about what adoption relationships were like. I think if we hadn't been through the process once before, we might have focused more on the prospect of adoption than on Sara herself. Since we had done that, and because we knew that adopting Caleb and Sara's child would also mean grafting them into our family tree, we were very interested in Sara as a person. We were obviously interested in the little one growing inside her eight-months-pregnant belly too, but our minds focused on what Sara would bring to our circle.

That was another thing—her eight-months-pregnant belly. Not only were we surprised to have been contacted within a month of finishing our paperwork, but Sara was only three weeks away from the day she was scheduled to be induced. When we adopted Ira, we were chosen about halfway through Brianna's pregnancy and we had a long time to worry about all the ups and downs. With Sara, we were on course to possibly go from paperwork to parenthood in just seven weeks. That would only happen if everything went through, of course, and we were far from certain that it would.

Our meeting left all of us hungry for more interaction. We set a time to meet up again the following week and we decided to do it at our house instead of at the agency office. Before we met Sara we were hesitant about the idea of a local birth parent having access to the inside of our home, but after we'd met her it was okay with us. Besides, having the meeting at our own home would give us the leisure to talk without worrying about the clock.

We scrubbed the house spotless and dressed Ira in some cute clothes in anticipation of her arrival. Things went pretty much like they had before, with conversation flowing easily and openly between us. She surprised us with an unexpected question, though. She said she noticed the six year age difference between Jammie and me, and wondered if there was something that had happened to create such a gap.

Of course there was, and the window to talk about my divorce was now open. I knew she of all people would understand, and she did. I don't go through my day everyday looking for ways to bring up my divorce, but it had been weighing on me ever since Sara had contacted us. I could see how heavy her recent divorce was on her shoulders, and I wanted to tell her she wasn't alone, that I understood a lot of what she was experiencing. Her question caught me off guard, but in the end it was nice to talk openly about it together.

Sara also brought up the topic of naming the child. She was pretty sure from the ultrasounds that the baby would be a girl, and she had thought of a couple names she liked, but she wanted us to name her if we were to be the parents.

Ira is a family name that comes from my father's side. It's my middle name, my grandpa's, and a few other relatives along my family line. We liked the idea of choosing another family name, which led us to choose the name Hazel, which is Jammie's mother's name. Sara was immediately on board with the name, and it was as simple as that.

Like many couples, Jammie and I had changed our minds a thousand times about the name before we got to the decision point, considering names long before we even turned in our paperwork, but by the time Sara asked us, we had chosen the one we liked. And since we enjoyed involving Brianna as a big part of choosing Ira's middle name, we encouraged Sara to choose a middle name for Hazel.

We enjoyed our visit and looked forward to doing it once more the following week, which would be the last full week before she was scheduled to deliver. This time, though, she asked if she could bring her mother along. We loved that idea.

Her mother wasn't completely on board with the idea of adoption. This wasn't something new to us since it had come up in conversation numerous times with Sara. Her mother wasn't the type of person to demand Sara do what she was told, though. She understood this was Sara's decision, but she was also under the impression that adoption would mean she wouldn't be able to have any contact with the child after placement.

Much of the world sees adoption that way—that the only two options are to see the child every day, or to never see her again. We tried to reassure her of our openness, but she thought it unlikely we would actually keep the adoption open.

We talked over dinner before Sara and Jammie went off to look at something together, leaving her mother and me together at the table.

At first I thought I was being clever by keeping her in conversation so Jammie and Sara could have some time alone. Jammie is better at deep heart-to-heart conversation than I am, especially with another woman, so I knew it was good for them to have some time together; it wasn't the first time I had slipped away to let them have that time. After a little while, though, I realized Sara's mom was doing the same thing with me: she was keeping me engaged in conversation so Sara and Jammie could have some time together.

Her mother knew Sara needed to make the decision for herself, but she also wanted to make sure she was making the decision for the right *reasons*. For instance, she offered to support her financially after the baby was born, if she chose to parent the child. I don't think she was trying to pressure her into parenting, I just think she just wanted to make sure Sara wouldn't regret her decision.

Before she left, Sara's mom expressed some emotions about how she was grateful we were in the picture. She was gaining a better understanding of what open adoption was like, and she could see how much we loved Sara. And by the time they drove away, we felt a much greater love and support from her.

We were glad to have been able to meet and start a relationship with Sara's mom. Many things were going our way, but we still weren't sure if Sara was going to choose adoption. We didn't want to pressure her, because we knew she would regret the decision if it was mostly someone else making it for her, but we could feel it: we were starting to get our hopes up. We felt like she would choose us to parent her child if she chose adoption—we just weren't sure she'd choose adoption.

Even though we weren't sure about everything, we finally decided it was time to start spreading the news. We had started to tell the rest of our close family about a week after we'd told Clark and Beth, but now we finally started telling the rest. We made sure everybody knew it wasn't a sure thing, but we wanted our friends to have a little notice rather than suffer the shock when we simply showed up one day with a baby. When we broke the news to Clark and Beth's kids, their four-year old got really sad. She didn't want the adoption to happen because she thought it meant we were going to trade Ira for the new baby, and she really loved him.

Brianna was the first person other than our siblings and parents to get the phone call, and she ran through her house screaming with excitement. She was beside herself with joy, knowing Ira could soon be a big brother.

We didn't talk about the process a whole lot on Facebook when we were going through our first adoption. Since we were connected to Brianna on Facebook from the very beginning, we refrained from posting a lot about the details of our adventure. We knew Brianna would be reading most of what we typed. Even when someone knows they are doing the right thing by choosing adoption, it is common to feel pain from the separation. We knew Brianna would be no exception, so we didn't want to rub it in by celebrating in front of her. We were glad we had Facebook with Brianna, though, since it was such a great tool to help us become acquainted.

Because we had the ability to see Sara face-to-face and didn't absolutely need to connect with her on the internet, we made no attempt to use social media with her at that time. Even though we took these precautions, the news spread through our social media networks like fire through desert grass. This time we were able to celebrate with all of our friends, and enjoy the interaction.

We knew celebrating a *possible* adoption meant that we might be setting ourselves up for a crash, but we were willing to take that risk. The possibility of welcoming a new addition into our home filled us with so much joy that we could no longer contain ourselves, even if we knew there was good chance it wouldn't happen.

We didn't think we would know for certain until at least a day or two after the child was born. All we could do was hope and pray Sara would make the right decision for her situation—whatever that decision would be—and to support her in it.

Chapter 6

The Moment Arrives

I sat home all morning with my little boy waiting for my phone to ring. Jammie had already gone to the hospital to be with Sara and her mom for the early stages of labor. I made some weak attempts at getting some work done, but there was no way my mind was ever going to be able to focus. I wasn't accomplishing anything.

My phone beeped. Jammie had sent me a text.

She was giving me a heads up that Caleb had come to the hospital and was there with them in the delivery room. I had known Caleb was going to come, but I didn't expect him to be there for a few more hours. The selfish part of me was hoping he would be too late for the delivery. I don't mean for that to sound cruel or insensitive, but his presence there worried me.

Part of the reason I was uneasy about him was because my divorce had ended with so many "what ifs."

After Amber had come back to town to finish school, and we had started spending some time around each other, our situation got much more complicated. I had such a hard time deciding what I wanted, and I could only imagine how difficult it would have been if some of that time had been together in a hospital delivery room.

I had been in Caleb's shoes before—sort of. Amber and I never had any children. I didn't know if his presence would cause drama between him and Sara, or drama between all of us. I didn't know how he felt about having us there. I didn't even know if he embraced the idea of adoption.

On top of all that were my prior experiences. Whenever the name of Ira's birth father came up, it was only because he was causing problems. My anxiety wasn't anything Caleb was responsible for, but my mind had an immediate aversion to the thought of a birth father being in the picture.

So when I got that text message from Jammie telling me Caleb was there at the hospital with them, my discomfort intensified. Everything was already complicated enough.

Jammie's next text told me she had spent the last little while chatting with and getting to know Caleb, and that I would like him. It didn't surprise me that she would say something like that. She knew I wasn't looking forward to spending the afternoon around him at the hospital, and her text message didn't change the way I felt.

I went back to my feeble attempt at making my morning productive, but I continued to fail miserably at it. Then the long-awaited phone call came.

It was time!

I quickly strapped Ira into his car seat and drove him to a friend's place to spend the day. En route, every car in front of me drove ten miles under the speed limit. Every time I passed one slowpoke I found myself stuck behind another one. Jammie called me a few times as I drove to tell me I'd better hurry.

I barely made it in time! The doctor was about to have Sara start pushing.

Jammie, Caleb, and Sara's mom stood in the room with the nurses and the doctor. I shook Caleb's hand, then we all went around the room and introduced ourselves. I later found out that the doctor made us do these introductions because he had been thinking all morning that Caleb was Jammie's husband, and he was confused who this big new bald guy was in the room.

We didn't feel right introducing ourselves as the couple who was going to adopt the baby, because we still didn't know if the adoption would take place. Sara still hadn't told us whether or not she was going to go through with it, so we just ended up saying that we were there to support them, and that if they chose adoption we would be the couple.

When it was Caleb's turn—he was the last in line to state his name—he said he was "Caleb, the real father."

That simple statement, "the real father," would normally have been a punch in the stomach. As soon as those words came out of his mouth though, Caleb reacted with discomfort so quickly that I immediately started to take a liking to him.

It wasn't that I enjoyed his discomfort, but seeing how he reacted to his own words helped me to see, immediately, that he cared about our feelings. He just didn't know yet what he was supposed to call himself. As Caleb appeared to search frantically for a better title than "the real father," Sara sent him a lifeline and said, "birth father." I saw Caleb subsequently mouthing the words to himself as if making mental notes on the terminology so that he could avoid running into that problem again.

My experience in Sara's delivery room was quite different from my experience with Brianna. Brianna gave birth at the largest hospital in Boise, while Sara chose a tiny hospital in a neighboring town. I had been at the hospital for about twelve hours by the time Brianna gave birth, but I popped in less than five minutes before Sara was told to start pushing.

One thing that was the same for both births, though, was my inability to calm my nerves. Even though I wasn't watching the actual delivery when Ira was born, I started to become faint almost as soon as Brianna started to push and I had to take a seat to avoid passing out. For some reason, my stubbornness to prove my machismo was taking over my rationale, and I insisted on staying on my feet for Hazel's birth. One of the nurses could see it written on my pale face and suggested I sit down, but I insisted on staying vertical. I don't know why it affects me so much, because I'm not scared or squeamish when I see blood. For some reason, just being in the room when a child is being born sucks the strength out of my knees.

I succeeded, though—sort of. Even with the nurse insisting every three minutes that I take a seat before passing out, my rump didn't touch a chair until baby Hazel made her debut into the world. The most beautiful baby girl I'd ever seen was born that hot summer day in a small town hospital.

The doctor and nurses quickly asked who was going to cut the cord, but that decision hadn't yet been made. I knew I was one of the candidates for the cutting ceremony, but I felt a little guilty about being the one to do it. I wasn't sure whether or not Hazel was ever going to come home with us and I didn't want to take that privilege away from someone else if I was going to be little more than a delivery room memory. They considered me and they considered Caleb, but I was happy and relieved when Sara asked her mom to do the honors. Truthfully, even though I thought it was fun to cut Ira's cord, I felt like having done it once was enough for me.

While everybody oohed, ahhed and marveled at the beauty of the world's newest citizen, I knew I had to find the nearest place to sit down. The climax of the experience proved to be a little too much for me and I was as close as I'd ever come to passing out. My stomach started to turn, my eyes started to glaze, and sweat flowed from every pore. Luckily though, as close as I came, I never did completely lose my grip on completely. I've still got my machismo.

Once my legs had recovered strength enough to stand, Jammie and I made our way over to the place where the nurses were cleaning Hazel up. I stared down at the beautiful baby girl as she cried, and I thought about all the possibilities if she were to come home with us.

The nurses were not at all used to a situation involving adoption. Delivery room congratulations were obviously part of their routine, but they didn't know exactly how to go about it. It would have been better if they had just saved their congratulations for another time, but the nurses repeatedly directed their congratulations toward us. We asked them every time not to because it was making everyone uncomfortable, but they just wouldn't stop.

After they had Hazel all cleaned up, they tried to hand her over to Jammie and me, but Jammie quickly pointed them toward Sara. It was Caleb and Sara's decision to make regarding who would hold her first, not ours. The last thing we wanted to do was to make them feel uncomfortable or pressured into doing something they didn't want to do.

We waited for a short while in the delivery room as Sara held the freshly swaddled baby in her arms. As tears slid down her cheeks, she stared into her baby's gray newborn eyes. Jammie and I knew what we needed to do, so we quietly excused ourselves from the room, giving them time alone. We went out to wait in the lobby without even touching baby Hazel.

Chapter 7

An Eventful Day

The little hospital didn't have a waiting room, so Jammie and I sat together on some chairs in a corner of the lobby, holding hands. Trying to sort through our thoughts was like trying to take a sip of water from a fire hydrant. So many emotions flooded our minds that it was impossible to organize our brains. We were so over-stimulated that all we could do was sit and rub each other's hands, staring into space.

Along with everything else that complicated our situation, Sara had been talking about breastfeeding Hazel while still at the hospital. Many people immediately think about the health benefits of receiving the mother's colostrum and milk, but Jammie and I focused more on the personal sides of the decision. Breastfeeding is an intimate bonding time between baby and mother, and Sara's desire to breastfeed made us think she was leaning toward raising Hazel, not choosing adoption. We didn't feel like it was our place to influence her either way so we left that decision up to her and Caleb.

While we sat quietly in our chairs studying the intricacies of the hospital lobby floor, Jammie asked me if I thought the adoption was going to go through. The answer came easily and quickly to my lips because it was something I'd been seriously considering for weeks: my answer was no. I didn't think it would go through. I had watched Caleb stand by Sara's side, holding her hand during the delivery. Sara had told us she was planning to breastfeed, which meant a lot of intimate bonding time. Plus, Sara would be at the hospital for forty-eight hours with Hazel, and most of that time they would be alone together. There were a lot of factors influencing the situation, so no; I didn't believe the adoption would go through. Jammie didn't either.

Jammie and I very much wanted another child, but decided at that moment that we'd better start coming to terms with the thought that Hazel wasn't going to be our daughter. Besides, even though we had gotten our hopes up, Sara had never promised us a thing, one way or another. We had no right to feel entitled to be Hazel's parents. The decision was not ours to make and we knew we needed to be there to support them in whatever decision they made, even if they didn't choose adoption. Adoptive couples shouldn't feel entitled to someone else's child simply because they want to be parents so badly.

With every minute that ticked away on the clock, I grew more and more convinced that I was right. I became certain during our time in the lobby that God was calling us to be part of Caleb and Sara's support group, but not to be Hazel's parents. That was going to take some mental adjustment.

We sat quietly in our little corner of the lobby for an hour and a half, which felt much longer than that. We didn't dare knock on their door or even peek our heads in. We quietly waited for someone to let us know what we should do.

Caleb eventually emerged from the delivery room with baby Hazel in his arms, wrapped in the familiar thin white hospital blanket with its pink and blue stripes. As he handed the little bundle of joy to Jammie, he told us Sara wanted us to be able to hold her, but he also asked us to stay in the lobby. She wasn't yet ready to see Hazel in our arms.

We were surprised when Caleb brought a small bottle of baby formula out for us to feed her. It was our first indication that Sara was no longer planning to breastfeed. Jammie and I took turns feeding Hazel.

Caleb sat with us. Even though I had been standing next to him most of the time in the delivery room, the circumstances had hardly given us time to have a conversation. Talk was a little slow and dry at first, but when we found that we both shared a love of playing guitar, words began to flow pretty easily between us. As we dabbled in other topics, we could feel he truly cared about us. It was refreshing to get to know the real Caleb. That helped me to toss out the imaginary one—the one who would only complicate things.

After about half an hour of holding Hazel in the lobby, Jammie asked Caleb to go into Sara's room to ask if she would like us to send Hazel back to her. When Caleb returned he told us that Sara wasn't ready to have her back. She also wasn't ready to see us holding her, so we stayed out in the lobby with Caleb while Sara stayed in her room with her mother.

After an hour had passed and she still hadn't asked for Hazel, Jammie asked Caleb to once again go to Sara, but this time she wanted him to ask if it would be okay for Jammie to come see her without Hazel. She said yes, so Jammie and Sara sat together in her room while Caleb and I stayed out in the lobby, talking about guitars, and taking turns holding Hazel.

After yet another hour, Jammie rejoined me in the lobby. The nurses decided to let us use one of the empty rooms rather than hang out in the public area. And even though nobody but hospital staff was present in the maternity wing that day, it was nice to have somewhere to retreat to.

Caleb offered to buy us dinner, which meant the world to us. We ate together in our own room while taking turns holding Hazel. Even though I had been dreading the thought of spending any time with Caleb just half a day earlier, I very much enjoyed having him around now. He spoke openly about how much he appreciated us and what we were doing, and we did our best to show him how much we appreciated him too. It was not only a nice change from our first adoption experience, but Caleb's presence was an added blessing.

Just as it had happened when Ira was born, a handful of family and friends called us, wanting to come to the hospital to see the new baby. We asked them all not to come though. The situation was simply too delicate. That, and Jammie and I felt like we were guests at the hospital. It didn't feel right to invite our friends and family to someone else's event. There would be plenty of time for them to see Hazel at our own home if she were to be ours.

When Hazel had first been brought out to us, we thought we would only be holding her for twenty minutes or so. We eventually stopped asking Sara whether she wanted us to bring her back because she repeatedly assured us that she would let us know. It wasn't until we'd had Hazel for four and a half hours that we looked up to see Sara shuffling into our room, walking very slowly, with a light smile on her face. We rushed to her and wrapped our arms around her.

Sara sat on the bed next to Caleb, opposite where Jammie and I were, and we offered Hazel to her. She turned the offer down. I was already in love with the little girl, but when Sara turned down the opportunity to take her from me, I felt an overwhelming rush of love and hope. Even though I had been holding little Hazel off and on for the last four and a half hours, the moment Sara said she would rather see Hazel in my arms than hold her was the first time I felt like I might be holding my daughter.

I pulled the sleeping baby girl into my chest as tightly as I could without waking her, and simply absorbed her presence. Sara still hadn't promised us she would choose adoption—and we had no right to feel entitled to Hazel—but in that moment I felt my bond with Hazel taken to a new level. At any time up to that point it would have hurt badly to have our adoption hopes stripped away, but that moment pushed me into a position where my heart would have been truly broken.

We talked lightheartedly about random topics, which eventually evolved into discussing Hazel's middle name. Sara asked us what we thought about calling her Hazel May. We loved it instantly. We not only loved the way it sounded, but we also loved that Sara had picked it out.

The evening began to get late, so Sara thanked Caleb for being there for her and hugged him goodbye for the night. He set off on his long drive home. Sara's sister then came and we continued to have fun visiting.

Sara still chose not to hold Hazel.

Eventually it was time for Jammie and me to head home for the night. Sara then took Hazel from our arms. It had been one of the most eventful days of our lives, and we left the hospital with an incredible amount of love for Caleb and Sara.

The next day we started off the morning by coming to see Sara and Hazel again. Sara was catching up on some much needed sleep when we got there, so we spoke mainly with her mother. We knew she was hurting from the thought of Hazel being raised in a different home. She teared up as she expressed her appreciation for how much we loved Sara. I was only able to stay for half an hour before heading to work, so I wasn't able to see Sara that morning. Jammie stayed for a few more hours, leaving early in the afternoon.

We had started the day filled with hope that we would be adding Hazel to our family. The previous night had ended on such an uplifting note that we couldn't help but feel optimistic about becoming parents again. As that second day progressed, though, our hopes sank again.

After Jammie left early that afternoon, Sara told her that she would call if she wanted us to come back for an evening visit. We waited anxiously all day and into the night with our phones in hand, ready to jump in the car and head to the hospital. Our hearts sank as we watched the evening get later and later without her calling. Our minds gravitated toward our fears of heartbreak.

We went to bed without receiving a phone call and without having any idea how Sara was doing. We wondered how tomorrow morning would go when Sara was scheduled to leave the hospital. We didn't know if Hazel May would be leaving the hospital with Sara, or if she would be coming home with us.

Chapter 8

A Temporary Goodbye

Even though we went to bed worried about what the next day would hold, waking up to a new day rejuvenated our hopes. We had expected a phone call the day before that didn't come. Our phones did ring the next morning while we were preparing to come to the hospital. It was Sara. She wanted to know if we could come earlier than we had originally planned. We hurried to drop Ira off at a friend's house and quickly made our way to the hospital.

Over the last two days, the nurses had often come to Jammie and me to ask questions about Hazel's treatment. They wanted to know from us what vaccinations she would be getting, but we insisted that they ask Sara. Over and over the hospital staff would get upset that we wouldn't make any of the decisions, but it wasn't our place to decide whether or not Hazel would get certain treatments and vaccines. We knew we could always have Hazel vaccinated later, after the adoption had gone through, if Sara had chosen not to do so.

Sara later told us how much that gesture meant to her, even though it made the relationship with the nurses frustrating.

After arriving—juggling our nerves and excitement—Jammie and I waited in an empty room while Sara and her caseworker went over some paperwork. We assumed Sara was planning to sign the papers since she had asked us to come early, but we were still extremely nervous as we quietly waited. The corny court TV show flickering on the television above us did nothing to help us pass the time.

We felt a lot of inner turmoil as we thought about Sara in the other room. It brought joy to our hearts to think of Hazel being a part of our family, but the act of signing the papers—the very thing that would make that possible—didn't signify party time for us. How could we jump up and down for joy in our room if we knew Sara was heartbroken in her room? Even if she knew what she was doing was right, we knew the separation would break her heart.

We knew Sara would come to us after her paperwork was finished, when she was ready, and we were willing to wait as long as she needed. Eventually Sara came in pushing Hazel's baby cart. Jammie and I immediately rushed over to her and we wrapped our arms around her again. We held each other for about a minute before letting go. We walked together back to Sara's room to gather the rest of Hazel's belongings before heading out.

When Sara asked if she could hold Hazel one last time, we told her "of course you can," assuring her that it certainly wouldn't be the last time.

She smiled an uneasy smile and held Hazel close to her.

When Sara handed Hazel back to us, we expected her gesture to be the climactic moment of the hospital experience—the last thing she did before we all left the hospital. We expected to immediately be able to slip Hazel into her car seat and head home, but the car seat was broken. We had inspected it before bringing it to the hospital, and it hadn't been very long since Ira had last used it, but we couldn't get it to work properly. We had said our emotional good-bye, but being forced to adjust and readjust the car seat forced us all to stand awkwardly together as we tried to sort the situation out. After 15 minutes of fiddling with the straps, the hospital told us they had a seat they could loan us.

Jammie and I carried Hazel to a room where the head nurse picked out a car seat for us to borrow, leaving Sara and her mom in their room. When we saw that the hospital was going to lend us a seat similar to the one Ira was currently using, I decided to run out to our car to check the sticker on it to see if it was suitable for a newborn.

As if the trouble with the car seat hadn't made our departure awkward enough, when I stepped out the side door of the storage room out into the parking lot, I happened to exit just as Sara and her mom came out of the hospital's front door. They had decided they were ready to leave and wanted to do so without another emotional goodbye. So when I emerged from the side door while they came out the front, it made the situation even more awkward. We smiled and waved from across the parking lot and they were on their way.

After we'd solved the problem with the car seat, I was outside bringing the car around. As Jammie was walking with Hazel toward the front doors, she was quickly stopped by a hospital worker who began questioning her about our little girl. After a handful of questions, Jammie realized that the worker was simply alarmed to see a newborn leaving the hospital with someone who obviously hadn't just given birth—she didn't know if Jammie was a baby snatcher or just a friend wanting to take the baby for a stroll.

Once Jammie realized what the issue was and explained the situation, they had a laugh together and we were on our way.

Hazel was in our care, but the adoption process had only just begun. The paperwork Sara had signed that morning did not relinquish her rights to the child. It only signed over temporary custody to the adoption agency, who in turn allowed us to care for Hazel. Caleb and Sara had the right to ask for Hazel back at any time.

We drove Hazel May to our home for the first time. We were in heaven.

I'd heard people say newborns can smile, but I never thought it actually happened. I always thought those parents were seeing what they wanted to see—that newborns only smiled by accident. But Hazel started smiling from the day she was born. She smiled in reaction to things going on in front of her and around her.

The biggest smile imaginable came across her perfect little lips the first time she was placed into her big brother's arms. Ira now had a little sister who was just seventeen months younger. Jammie and I were beginning to feel like we had a daughter, but there was so much to do and still time to pass before everything would be final.

We snapped a bunch of photographs during those first few days, but we didn't send any of them to Sara. Jammie and Sara had discussed the exchange of photos and decided Sara would let us know when it was okay to start sharing them with her. She wanted to take some time away for herself. We told her just to heal at her own pace and to let us know when she was ready.

There was a lady who began to stick her nose into the situation. She knew a lot about adoption and was in regular contact with both us and Sara. When she called Jammie to give her a hard time about not sending Sara any pictures, we began to second-guess the way we had been handling things. On the one hand, Sara had asked us not to send pictures and preferred we give her some space for a little while. On the other hand, there weren't very many people talking to both sides, and this lady was telling us Sara needed pictures.

Our relationship with Sara during those first few days was emotional and delicate. We didn't want to do anything to overstep our bounds or make her uncomfortable.

Even though Sara had asked us to wait for her to contact us first, after giving it some thought, Jammie decided to send Sara a text message to ask her about pictures. Sure enough, Sara wrote back saying she wasn't ready yet.

After a few more days Sara texted us again, apologizing about not feeling ready for close contact. We were confused about why she would feel the need to do that. We reassured her that the only thing we wanted was for her to be able to heal at her own pace and in her own way. If she wanted photos, that was fine. If she wanted to come visit, that was good too. If not, we were okay with that as well.

We later found out that the same lady who had given Jammie a hard time about not sending photos had also questioned Sara's choice to keep her distance. This lady told her that most women wouldn't be hurting so badly so soon after the hospital and that the pain usually came later.

The nerve of that lady! If there's one thing I've learned when talking about adoption with other people, it's that there is nothing universal about the feelings associated with the process. Everybody experiences things differently. That's true for everybody involved—whether on the adoptive side or the biological side. So, for this woman to tell Sara that the hurt she was feeling was misplaced—especially at a point in time when she was so vulnerable to another's opinion—was completely out of line. We assured Sara that she was not only justified in wanting to heal at her own pace and in her own way, but also that the hurt she was feeling was normal.

We had gone through the adoption process once before, but things were very different this time. Just like we had done the first time around, we were again learning as we went.

Brianna had come over for her first visit the day after Ira came home with us, and Sara didn't want to do that. Brianna wanted a lot of pictures and contact, especially in those early days after placement, but Sara didn't. But we were more than willing to roll with the changes in order to give Sara the tools she needed to adjust. We wanted her to be comfortable with her circumstances in order to build together the foundation of our open adoption relationship.

It didn't happen immediately like it had with Brianna, but Sara did eventually contact us, asking if she could visit.

Chapter 9

The First Few Weeks

A little before Hazel turned two weeks old, Sara asked us for pictures, which we were happy to share. A few days after that, Sara asked if she could come for a visit. We had been talking with her a little via phone and text, but we didn't completely know what to expect.

When Brianna had come for her first visit, things were very difficult. She was very emotional and really struggled with putting Ira down when it came time for her to go. After Brianna left, we were very worried she was going to change her mind.

We didn't know if Sara's first visit would be similar—if she was going to have a hard time putting Hazel down. We weren't sure if Sara was only interested in seeing Hazel, or if she would also want to see Jammie, Ira, and me. We wondered whether or not the visit would be uncomfortable, but we had never let a little fear of discomfort scare us away from anything adoption related before, so we were happy to invite her over.

There were a few uncomfortable moments, but they were very minor. Overall I think it went rather well. There were a lot of smiles to accompany the tears as we talked. We stayed up late, enjoying our conversation. It had never been a problem, especially between Jammie and Sara, to talk openly about difficult and intimate feelings.

Throughout the entire evening I noticed Hazel was getting passed freely between Jammie and me, but Jammie was never offering to let Sara hold her. That confused me. It wasn't like Jammie to refrain from letting Sara cuddle her. Since most of the communication before the visit had been just between the two women, it seemed like a good idea to follow Jammie's lead throughout the evening.

After dinner and hours of conversation, I finally offered Sara what Jammie wasn't: I asked her if she would like to hold Hazel.

Both Jammie and Sara laughed. It wasn't until that moment that they realized they'd forgotten to tell me what they had discussed: we wouldn't offer for Sara to hold Hazel. Instead, we would wait until Sara asked to hold her. Since there had been times at the hospital when Sara had preferred not to hold her, Jammie didn't want her to feel obligated now if she wasn't ready. She was welcome to ask for her at any time. That made sense. Hazel wasn't being kept away from Sara. Sara just needed a little more time.

All of Sara's early visits were similar to that first one. We spent the majority of the time in our home talking. Sara didn't choose to hold Hazel very often, and even when she did, she would usually only hold her for a few minutes at a time before handing her back to one of us. If there was one thing I was grateful for, it was that Sara was both able and willing to express what she wanted and needed. She was able to be straightforward with us.

Our relationship was still developing, but we felt comfortable enough to ask her if she wanted to do a photo shoot with us. Shortly after Ira was born, before Brianna had flown back to Mississippi, we took some really nice photos together. Those were displayed on our walls at home and are some of the most cherished photos we have.

We didn't get the opportunity to include Ira's birth father in those pictures, but Hazel's birth father was much more involved in her adoption. As a result, we thought we should ask both Caleb and Sara if they would like doing a photo shoot with us. They agreed.

It was a little difficult to arrange a time since Caleb was living on the other side of the state, but eventually we were able to set it up. We went to the home of one of Jammie's photographer friends and set up in her home studio.

The pictures turned out amazing, but the aftermath wasn't. In hindsight I reflected on how I would have felt if I had been asked to do a photo shoot with Amber a few months after our divorce.

The problem with the situation wasn't that it put Caleb and Sara back into communication with one another. They had been talking with each other regularly over the past few weeks, which was part of what made us think they would be comfortable doing the shoot together. The problem was what a photo shoot represented.

Every photo was a portrait of what Caleb and Sara had wanted to build when they got married. The click of the camera was forcing them to reminisce about the hopes and dreams they once had together. The feelings that had been churned up by their time together at the hospital and the weeks following, all came to a head that day.

They seemed to be comfortable next to each other before we started taking pictures, but by the end of the shoot the obvious discomfort was overwhelming.

Jammie and I were terrified after that photo session.

We had planned for a short visit before Caleb would need to drive home, so we drove back to our house. Jammie and I quickly brainstormed about how we could help extinguish the uncomfortable feelings our photo shoot had ignited, but when Caleb and Sara decided not to come into our house, we became lost in what to do.

Jammie and I walked into the house, but Caleb and Sara stayed in their car. They needed some time alone to discuss things.

Hazel was a few weeks old by this time and we'd spent every minute since she was born growing more in love with her. We knew that there were still a lot of things that needed to happen before an adoption would be final, but we felt bonded to her as if she had been born to us. The fear of losing that, even if we had no right to feel entitled to her, was overwhelming. Caleb and Sara were within their rights to change their minds at any moment and Hazel would no longer be in our home.

Jammie and I sat in the living room as we watched them sitting in Caleb's car. Flashbacks of watching Caleb hold Sara's hand at the hospital made me wonder if they were considering giving their relationship another try. I knew what it felt like to consider those feelings since I had gone through something similar with Amber.

And even if they didn't rekindle their relationship, we wondered if they were contemplating whether or not to change their mind about adoption.

It was not our place to tell them what they should do. I had enough people give me unsolicited input during my divorce to know that they were the only ones who could truly know what was best for them.

There was only one thing Jammie and I could do, and that was sit and watch the black Chevy through the bay windows of our living room. Jammie held Hazel tightly to her chest, unable even to put her down for her much-needed nap. She sat in her rocking chair, holding little Hazel May as tightly as she could, and I paced the floor, keeping my eyes out on the curb where her biological parents were parked.

That's all we did for nearly an hour.

Finally, their doors opened and they stepped out onto the sidewalk. We watched as Caleb walked around to where Sara was standing, and wrapped his arms around her. They separated and Sara walked straight to her own car. Caleb watched her drive away then he made his way to our front door.

We had a million questions in our mind, but we weren't sure if it was our place to ask any of them. Once Caleb was seated on our couch, though, we had to at least ask something, or we would go out of our minds with worry. Caleb confirmed they had been discussing what to do with their relationship and adoption, but said that they decided not to get back together.

His words didn't completely relieve all our worries, but we were able to exhale for the first time in nearly an hour. We talked for only about ten more minutes before hugging him goodbye and seeing him off. Before he left we gave him the gift we had picked out for him: a pair of cuff links—one with Hazel's initials on it and the other with her birth date. We had already given Sara her gift—a locket with a picture of Hazel in it. These gifts weren't much, but hopefully they were something the two of them could cherish for a long time.

We had hope that we were on a path that would lead us to being parents again. Still, our bumpy road had a major hurdle. If the adoption was ever going to become finalized, Caleb and Sara would have to sign papers in front of a judge. In Idaho that process normally takes only a week or two, but Caleb and Sara's caseworker seemed to be dragging her feet on purpose and we didn't know why.

Chapter 10

Transition to a New Life

Brianna had appeared in front of a judge about one week after Ira was born. That court appearance was only for Brianna since Jammie and I wouldn't have our turn in front of a judge for months to come. Brianna's court appearance was only to relinquish her parental rights and transfer custody to the adoption agency. Things were different with Sara.

More and more time continued to pass, and Caleb and Sara still hadn't made their appearance in front of a judge. The caseworker who was responsible for scheduling that seemed to be dragging her feet, apparently on purpose.

She hadn't specifically told us the reasons why she hadn't made any effort to arrange a court date. As we pieced together the conversations we'd had with her, it became logical to conclude that she wanted to be sure that Caleb and Sara had enough time to make a good decision and not regret it. After all, even though Hazel came home with us from the hospital, Sara still hadn't verbalized her decision to place with us. We assumed by her actions that she was leaning toward going through with the adoption, but she hadn't confirmed that yet.

It was torture for everyone to sit in limbo, baby Hazel in our arms, but not see any progress on the legal side. Every day we worried it might be our last day with Hazel. We constantly wondered whether or not Caleb and Sara would get back together, which we assumed would mean that Hazel would return to them. Every moment with Hazel meant we were falling more in love with her, all the while becoming more afraid that our hopes would be dashed.

I'm not sure how that stretch of time weighed on Caleb, but we did talk with Sara about it. It was just as heavy on her shoulders as it was on ours, and we could imagine what she was going through: every morning she would awaken to a new day knowing the child that had grown inside of her was living in a different home. And knowing that it wasn't too late to change her mind, every day Sara had to make that difficult decision again about whether or not to choose adoption. Every day she renewed her decision, but from our vantage point, making the same decision each day made it harder, not easier. It wore on her.

Finally, after five weeks without a court date, we called Jon—our own caseworker—and asked him what was holding things up. He was surprised that it hadn't been taken care of, and when he called us back later that day he said it was a good thing we called when we did. He and Sara's caseworker were able to schedule a time in court almost immediately. If we hadn't called that day it would have taken at least a few more weeks.

During those five weeks after Hazel's birth, Sara had been making a number of trips back and forth to eastern Idaho. She wanted to get back to the same university she had been attending before she and Caleb separated. She also needed a job, and she hoped to get her old job back. She would have to move back near Caleb if she was going to get her old life back.

During this period of time, Sara came to me on a few occasions to talk about my past with Amber. She wanted to know what regrets I had, how I overcame certain difficulties, and what factors I considered when Amber and I began to spend time around each other again. It was very hard for me to remain neutral during those conversations since restarting her relationship with Caleb would likely mean changing her mind about adoption, but that was exactly what I needed to do.

I liked both Caleb and Sara—if they wanted to get back together, who was I to say it was a bad idea? After all, one of my closest friends at the time of my divorce went through something very similar, except that he and his ex-wife did reunite and they are perfectly happy to this day. I knew quite a bit about what she was going through generally, but I couldn't begin to pretend my situation was exactly like hers. My decisions regarding Amber would have been much more difficult if there had been a child involved.

Jon had set up a court date for Caleb in eastern Idaho first. We were finally taking the next step, which would soon be followed by Sara making a court appearance.

Jon called us that morning after Caleb's appointment in court and we were given a wonderful surprise. Since Sara happened to be in eastern Idaho at the time, and since she had already been talking with Caleb, she decided to go with him to court. They both signed at the same time. We thought it would be nearly a week before Sara would get that chance.

We later found out that Caleb and Sara sat together for hours that morning talking about whether or not they wanted to go through with it. They had made up their minds before, but this court appearance would make their decision final.

If Jammie and I had known they were together that morning deciding whether or not to change their minds, we would have been pacing in our home, emotional wrecks. Since we didn't even know Sara was in eastern Idaho at the time, we had been going about our day as usual.

We felt an immediate uplift in Sara's spirits from that day on. Now that she no longer had to make the same adoption decision over and over again, she was able to focus harder on her goal of getting back into her routine.

She wasn't able to get her old job back and she needed to find work as soon as possible. I hadn't realized it at first, but her expertise was in the same field as what my cousin, Devin, did, and he needed to hire someone. Devin was one of the owners of a hospice company, which was right up Sara's alley. I called him and before long she was sitting across from him to interview for a job. She started out part-time, but soon went to full-time. Getting this job in Boise meant that she wasn't going to be moving back to eastern Idaho, but she was okay with that. She also transferred her credits to the local university and continued her schooling here.

Devin was an interesting fit into our circle because he was a birth father, but not really by choice. He was once married and, just like Caleb and Sara, found out he was going to be a dad about the time he separated from his wife. Devin's ex-wife did everything in her power to exclude him from his daughter's life. After years of legal struggles and frustrations, Devin eventually agreed to allow his daughter to be adopted by her new stepfather. Devin and I were college roommates throughout the majority of that time and I saw firsthand how it tore him apart.

Jammie and I have always enjoyed open relationships with our children's biological families. We have even grown close to some of the extended family of our children's birth parents. Up until this point, however, we've never had our own extended family interact with our adoptive families. Brianna got to know some of our family while she was living here, but they don't have an ongoing relationship.

We were excited to see Sara with a good job, but we didn't know whether or not her relationship with Devin would complicate things. We knew our relationship with Sara would have its ups and downs. If things began to go badly at work, would it affect our relationship with Sara since Devin and I are so close? Would the difficult times in our adoption relationship make it awkward for her at work?

Our worries turned out to be nothing. Her new job only helped our relationship as she worked at getting back into the swing of things.

Sara continued to visit often. We grew closer with each visit. Sara still didn't hold Hazel very much, but their bond grew every time she came over.

Even though we had adopted once before, having a birth parent live nearby was something we had never experienced. A lot of our experiences were brand new to us. Most of the time we spent getting to know Brianna was before Ira was born. After Ira came into our home and our relationship changed, we continued working on our relationship from 2,000 miles away.

We didn't have much time to get to know Sara before Hazel was born, but she lived conveniently close and we were able to spend a lot of time together after placement.

Our situation with Caleb was different. We didn't get to know him at all before meeting him at the hospital and although he didn't live as far away as Brianna, he did live on the other side of the state. We'd been able to visit with him a few times when he was in town, but we decided it was time to take a trip out to eastern Idaho to visit him at his home.

Chapter 11

Our New Extended Family

We called Caleb to see if we could come spend an afternoon with him. He was excited and asked if it would be okay to invite some of his family too. We liked that idea and we were excited to meet them.

Car trips had become more complicated now that we had two kids in diapers. We arrived at Caleb's house much later than we had told him we would. When I pulled Ira out of his car seat, I didn't realize he had spent the last hour sitting on a really sticky piece of candy. Pulling him out of his seat and holding him close to me slimed my shirt with red goo all the way down my front. And that was nothing compared to the state Ira's clothes were in. It was a warm sunny day, so we stripped him down to his diaper right there on the street and put some fresh clothes on him.

Caleb saw us pull up, and he came out to help sort out the chaos before welcoming us inside. I couldn't believe my eyes as I stepped into his living room. Jammie and I were expecting to see Caleb's parents and maybe a brother or two, but there was also Hazel's birth great-grandma, a handful of aunts and uncles, a great aunt, and some cousins. Caleb's small apartment was completely full of people anxiously waiting for our arrival and excited to meet Hazel. We felt like celebrities walking in a parade with so many people excited to see us, with all of the love and admiration radiating our way.

People took turns feeding, burping, and snuggling Hazel. We had expected that, but we didn't expect the amount of interest they also had in the rest of us. Sure, they all wanted their turn holding the new little baby, but when it wasn't their turn to hold her, they were just as excited to get to know Jammie, Ira, and me.

They brought gifts for Ira as well as for Hazel. We appreciated him being included like that.

We visited late into the afternoon. As Hazel continued to get passed around, Caleb and I each grabbed one of his guitars and started jamming together. It was fun to finally be able to play together since we had spent so much time talking about it.

A few weeks later we decided to go visit Jammie's brother, and since the trip would take us through that part of eastern Idaho we asked Caleb if he'd like to meet somewhere for dinner. We met for a few hours at a restaurant and enjoyed the evening together.

All of our contact with our children's birth families had always been on such a small scale up to that point—one person here and one person there—that I hadn't let it soak in just how many people were emotionally invested in our adoptions. Even though I had met some of both Brianna's and Sara's families before—in person as well as online—being surrounded by so many people at one time really opened my eyes to the magnitude of it all.

Hazel was the first grandchild in Caleb's family. When his mom thanked us over and over again for letting them get a chance to hold her and be part of her life, we were surprised. We had told them we would be doing that, but she said she didn't think someone would actually follow through with something like that.

We had already learned to love a birth mother through our first adoption, but having a birth father in our loving circle was an amazing bonus. When we adopted Ira, because of how things were with his birth father, we worried ourselves sick all the way up to the day the adoption was finalized. After Caleb and Sara had their day in court, we didn't have much to stress about. Jammie and I still had a few months before we would see a judge, but we were able to spend that time getting to know Caleb and Sara better, rather than worry about the adoption falling through.

Our day in court came when Hazel was about three months old.

We expected the judge to be stern and to lecture us. That's how it was when we adopted Ira. The judge for Hazel's adoption smiled the entire time we were with her. She was fascinated by the concept of open adoption and spent more time asking questions to satisfy her own curiosity than she did with the actual adoption proceedings. She celebrated our adoption right along with us. Court wasn't serious and stern this time—it was fun.

I don't think the security guard thought it was quite so much fun, though. He about shut the whole building down when he found what he thought might be a bomb left by the entrance. That was my fault. I put the diaper bag down by the entrance of the building and left it unattended while we were out taking pictures. Oops.

After the adoption was finalized, our relationship with Caleb and Sara continued to grow. Sara's visits were usually similar—spending most of the time sitting around talking, laughing, and eating dinner. Even after three months she still didn't want to spend much time holding Hazel. That was okay. We wanted her to develop a relationship with Hazel in her own way.

Jammie once asked Sara if being around Hazel made it hard. Her response surprised me. Sara said that because three-month-old Hazel looked so different from three-day-old Hazel, that it was like they were different kids. The more Hazel changed physically, the easier it became. I hadn't thought of that before.

Then a few weeks after the adoption was finalized, Sara came for a visit and we talked about something that had been on her mind. Her social life wasn't where she wanted it to be and she thought it might help if she created some distance between us. Her life over the past year had been consumed by divorce and adoption. She hoped that having some time away would clear her mind since over the last year she had thought about little more than divorce and adoption.

The change wouldn't be permanent. It would be just until she felt like her personal life was back on track. Until she contacted us, we wouldn't call or send text messages. Most importantly, she wouldn't be coming to our home.

We were proud of her for making that decision—not because we were relieved to have her gone, but because she was taking charge of her own circumstance and working through things in her own way. Since one of our main goals with open adoption has always been to give the birth parents the tools they need to heal, we were happy to adapt to these changes. That has always been a big part of what open adoption has meant to us—being open to change.

Although she wasn't going to be calling or visiting, she still wanted us to share pictures with her.

Sharing pictures with birth parents used to be difficult for us. When Ira was young and we were developing our relationship with Brianna, we felt insecure in our role as adoptive parents. Posting pictures felt like we were reporting to Brianna. Giving her a chance to peek into our home made us feel like we were being examined. The thought of being examined was uncomfortable because, if we felt like we had to report to someone about how things were going, then it was like someone was above us in the pecking order. If there were people above us in hierarchy, then were we really the parents?

Once we had ironed out many of the wrinkles in our relationship with Brianna, we grew a lot more comfortable in our role with her. We weren't just proud to be parents, we were also proud to say we were part of the adoption world. When we saw how Brianna supported and sustained us in what we were doing, we stopped feeling so insecure. We no longer felt like we were being audited and it felt more like we were sharing something special with someone we love. I think that's the way it should be.

Since we had already worked out the majority of those insecurities with Brianna, sharing photos with Caleb and Sara wasn't difficult.

Jammie had created a special blog just for Brianna when Ira was born. Choosing to post on a blog rather than send pictures through email or the postal service was beneficial in a lot of ways. Brianna could check the site at her own leisure. She could leave us responses along with the posts. She was able to give the blog password to select family and friends so that they could stay updated too. And since Jammie is a photographer who takes very nice photos, Jammie could post them in full resolution rather than shrink them to fit an email or Facebook post. Brianna could print any of the photos at high quality.

After talking to Caleb and Sara, Jammie decided it would be best to create separate blogs. Caleb and Sara were no longer spending time together and both wanted to move on. If they shared a blog, they and their family members would be able to leave comments under each post. We worried it would make them uneasy to be interacting again that way. The last thing we wanted was for their blog to be an uncomfortable place to go.

So Jammie organized and updated three separate blogs—for Brianna, Sara, and Caleb. Yes, that was a lot of work. Even though Jammie was able to cut and paste most of the information and pictures so that the blogs were pretty much the same, it took a lot of time.

We tried this kind of appeasement for months, having never intended to keep it that way forever. It came to its inevitable end when we accidentally posted pictures of our visit to Caleb's house on Sara's site.

We then decided it was time to simplify things. We stopped maintaining three separate blogs and merged them into one. We kept our posts neutral, refraining from posting pictures with birth parents, knowing that we could always email those pictures separately.

Chapter 12

Another Visit from a Familiar Face

Sara told us she would contact us when she was ready to start visiting again, but we didn't know how long that might be. Jammie and I wondered every day how she was doing. We worried about her because we cared, but we still honored her wishes and kept our distance.

Sara stayed away for two months before coming over to visit again. Having some time away served her well. She was doing great at her job and made some new friends. She told us it was nice not to think about whether or not she wanted to visit, which enabled her to go about her day without being consumed by adoption. When she started visiting us again she glowed even more than before.

We had asked Brianna on multiple occasions whether or not she wished we lived closer together. She had considered coming out west to go to college, but the more she thought about it, the more she liked having the distance between us. She came to visit around Ira's first birthday, and although there were some difficult emotions during that visit, she loved it. She decided that visiting about once a year would be perfect for her.

Before Brianna's first visit, we stressed about all the things that could have gone wrong. Since that visit went so well we were excited to find out she was coming again after Ira's second birthday.

She had always shown us that she approved of our parenting and sustained us as "Mom and Dad," so we were able to let go of our insecurities and truly look forward to her visit.

She was still in high school, so we had originally thought about having her stay for a whole week during spring break, but that plan changed: she would fly in late Friday and leave early Monday, staying for a few days over Easter weekend.

Ira had already been asleep for hours when her flight arrived, but she was still excited to see him. It was fun to see her peek in on him to watch him sleep.

Brianna had a lot of fun playing with Ira in the morning as well as getting to know Hazel for the first time. She had been dying to meet her ever since she was born.

Along with being excited to see Ira and Hazel, Brianna wanted to visit with Virginia. Virginia led a birth mother support group, and every week when Brianna was pregnant and living with us, she attended it. They were anxious to see each other again, so we planned to meet for breakfast that morning.

Even though we had known Brianna for about two and a half years by that point, and she knew us intimately, we still felt the need to prove ourselves as good parents. We wanted to show her with every parental act that she made a good decision when she chose us. She always sustained us, but we found ourselves constantly wanting to prove her right.

I was first out the door with Ira and I strapped him into his car seat. As soon as I shut his door and turned to make my way to the driver seat, I heard the familiar click of the door locks. I turned back around and saw that I had left my keys in Ira's hand.

He had just pressed the lock button on the keychain. We didn't have a spare. Jammie and I took turns trying to get him to press the unlock button on the keychain, but to no avail. Ira spent ten minutes popping the trunk and making the car honk, but he never pressed the right button. He eventually dropped the keys on the floor.

Waiting for the locksmith to come made us about an hour late for breakfast with Virginia. Brianna was able to laugh about the situation, but it sure wasn't my brightest moment. Getting the kids ready for breakfast and into the car was one of my first parental acts during her visit and I blew it!

We planned a busy day, which included a trip to the aquarium in Boise. It was a fun activity, but the ride back home sparked a dramatic change in the visit. Ira was very tired by that point, and like most two year olds, when he gets tired he gets cranky. His chosen expression of rebellion was to repeatedly kick his baby sister in her car seat. When he was reprimanded he started the biggest tantrum he had ever thrown. He kicked and screamed at the top of his lungs the entire half hour drive home. Brianna was sitting right by him in the back seat the whole time. She was about as uncomfortable as she could be.

Jammie has always been awesome with Sara and Brianna. She has a connection with them that I will never have. Once we got back home, Jammie could see the discomfort written all over Brianna's face. They knew it was time for a talk.

The last time Brianna had seen Ira, he wasn't even able to walk yet, let alone talk, so most of Brianna's communication was with Jammie and me. Now that Ira was two years old, he was much more capable of interacting with her. He didn't have to roll and crawl anymore because he could walk, jump, and run. He was able to say words, including her name, which sounded a lot like Banana. He would come up to her, hug her, or jump onto her lap. He was growing up and he was doing it without her there.

Brianna and Jammie talked about something difficult that happened right before going to the aquarium. Jammie wanted to change Ira's diaper before leaving. She called for Ira to "come to Mom." When Ira saw the diaper in Jammie's hand, he ran to Brianna's leg and latched on in hopes to avoid a diaper change. So when Jammie told him to come to Mom, Ira ran straight for Brianna. That sparked some intense emotions that were only fueled later by the discomfort of Ira's backseat temper tantrum.

Brianna and Jammie sat talking in the back room for a long time. Eventually, Sara showed up and we all ate dinner together. We laughed together as we took a step back and looked at our situation. Many people think we're crazy for letting our children's biological parents be such a big part of our lives. Sitting around the table with birth moms from both of our adoptions showed how unusual our family tree is, but it has become normal to us. Our home is unique and we love it.

The next day was Easter, and Brianna went to church with us. She had gone with us a lot back when she was pregnant, so she was able to see some people with whom she had become friends.

One lady, Sharon—who was in town visiting her daughter—had heard about our adoptions and was eager to ask Jammie some relevant questions. Her daughter had just finished her paperwork; she was waiting to be chosen to adopt. She was especially struggling with the concept that her daughter wanted to parent through open adoption. She struggled to see the benefits of an open relationship. As she asked these questions, she didn't realize that the girl sitting next to her, Brianna, was the same birth mom Jammie was talking about. They laughed together when Jammie pointed her out. It was a fun coincidence that this lady had come to visit the same weekend as Brianna. She was able to see firsthand how close, loving, and healthy the relationship can be between an adoptive mom and a birth mom.

After church, Brianna and Jammie packed up all of Jammie's photography equipment and drove downtown for a photo shoot. They had already been planning to take Brianna's high school senior portraits even before Brianna arrived, but didn't realize when they planned just how big of a blessing that time together would turn out to be.

Brianna loved Ira. There was absolutely no doubt in any of our minds about that. Still, she needed a break. Having some quality woman-to-woman time together gave Brianna a chance to relax.

There were a few stressful times, especially for Brianna, but the visit was fantastic. Just like when she had come a year earlier, our relationship with Brianna was brought to a new level. Her relationship with Ira grew as well. It's hard to know how often she'll be able to visit over the years, and how often we'll be able to go to Mississippi to see her, but we're always excited when we get a chance to be together. Our door will always be open to her.

Chapter 13

Touched by Adoption

In the time I have spent as an advocate for open adoption, the question I am asked the most is just how open an adoption relationship should be. It's an intimidating thought for hopeful adoptive parents to ponder. Just like any other kind of relationship, it takes time. That's the most important thing to consider.

Nobody, including the adoption agency, ever told us what our relationship should be like. We invite our children's birth parents into our home because we know it's right for us. A lot of people think we're too open with our children's birth parents. Others think we should be willing to share even more than we do. Those people aren't in our home and their opinions aren't important to us. Jammie and I are the parents and we are the ones God put in this position to make those decisions, not anybody else.

Sometimes, like it happened with our children's birth parents, relationships blossom quickly. We only needed to sit down with Sara once before we felt comfortable inviting her to our home. When we thought of the option of having Brianna fly out to stay with us, we hesitated for just a moment to give it thought and then smiled at the idea. We accompanied all of our decisions with a lot of prayer and God was with us every step of the way.

I usually recommend that people start their adoption relationships out slowly—with things they are sure they are comfortable with. It's much easier to start out somewhere safe and secure, not putting too much on the table, and to let things develop progressively. Going backward, starting out with an open relationship then closing some of the communication, is difficult and dangerous to the relationship.

When we were first contacted by Brianna, we didn't understand much of what we were getting into. We knew we wanted an open adoption, but we were probably too quick to promise so much. We knew what our pre-birth relationship was like, but we didn't realize how it would change.

Before Ira was born, Brianna had all the "power" in the relationship. I don't mean to say she was pushing us around and calling the shots, but at any moment she could have changed her mind. There would have been nothing we could have done about it.

After Ira was born and the adoption was final, we were the ones in position to call the shots. If at any time we wanted to close the adoption, it would have been within our right to do so; there would have been nothing she could have done about it. The balance of power shifted—the roles swapped. Even during the hard times we've loved having a relationship with Brianna, so cutting her off from contact is not something we've ever considered. Our love for her and her family has always outweighed any of our insecurities.

When had already learned, before we met Caleb and Sara, that it would be a bad idea to quickly promise them the world. Even as our relationship was budding and we were figuring things out together, we didn't know what it would be like after Hazel was born. There was no way for us to know, even though we'd been through it once before with Brianna. We did make promises, but we kept them simple. We promised them we would never cut them off from contact and we promised we would always be open to discussing what was best for everybody involved.

Also, when we first met them we had a better understanding about the role they would play in our family. Brianna, Caleb, and Sara don't care only about the children; they care about us as a family. None of them visit just to hold the child to whom they gave birth. Actually, in difficult times it seemed like holding Hazel was a safe refuge for Brianna, even though she didn't give birth to her. It seemed to be the same for Sara when she held Ira.

Our relationships have continued to evolve and we all know that going through different stages in life will mean our relationships could always take different turns. It's likely that Sara, Brianna, and Caleb will all be married with families of their own someday. Our relationships are mostly based on what we grownups think is best, but someday Ira and Hazel will be able to better understand their situation and will make decisions for themselves. Ira and Hazel may not even want the same thing as one another. Who knows? That's the essence of an open adoption. We're all open to change. We're all open to what other people might need or want. We're all open-minded.

Hindsight has shown me just how much God has guided us through our adoptions. I wasn't able to see many of the blessings we received at the time, but looking back I can see them plainly.

My divorce from Amber was the most difficult thing I have ever gone through in my life. It beat my emotions up to the point where there were times when I wondered if I would ever feel happy or normal again. But those experiences have ended up being some of my greatest blessings. Although I have always appreciated Brianna, I had never been able to directly relate to her situation. Caleb and Sara went through something so similar to my own experience that I was better able to ask myself what it would be like to be in their shoes. The jump between our circumstances wasn't as far as the leap I had to take in order to relate to Brianna when she was giving birth at age fifteen. I've asked myself countless times how I would feel and react if Amber had been pregnant and wanted to choose adoption. It's helped me see better just how difficult that decision must have been for our children's birth parents. My past has helped me to better appreciate not only Caleb and Sara, but also Brianna.

I don't doubt God guided us in every step of our journey and He will continue to do so throughout our lives. I don't believe it was a coincidence that our paths crossed with Caleb and Sara. If we had been just a few weeks slower in deciding to adopt again, or if we had been slower with our adoption paperwork, Hazel would be in someone else's arms.

I trust God. I trust He would have led Caleb and Sara to another loving home if we weren't ready to adopt again. I'm really glad we were ready, though, and grateful God saw us as a good fit with Caleb, Sara, and Hazel. I think we are all a great fit together. Our relationship wasn't automatic, but it did develop quickly because both sides were willing to share what we truly needed and felt. I'm grateful that Caleb and Sara were willing to let God guide them to us.

When I take a step back, I see just how many people have been directly touched by our situation. My family and close friends, as well as people connected with Caleb and Sara, will never look at family or adoption the same way. Adoption changes people and it changes lives. One of my goals in life is to help Ira and Hazel see how much love they have brought into the world because of their adoption history and because of who they are. I want them to grow up embracing their past. Whether they choose to speak as freely about adoption as Jammie and I do will be up to them, but in the end they will know just how special they are to all of us.

Jammie and I have benefitted greatly from our relationships with Brianna, Caleb, and Sara. We didn't choose open adoption for ourselves, though. We chose it for our children. As they grow up, their understanding will deepen and they will know that their birth parents made their decisions out of love. They will grow up experiencing that love firsthand because they will know their birth parents personally. They will be able to see Jammie and me demonstrate that love for their birth parents. The best way to teach love is always by example.

Now that I have Jammie, Ira, and Hazel, I have everything I've always wanted. All those years I spent being hungry for the things my brother had are now past; Ira and Hazel have made my life full. I don't know if Jammie and I will ever have another child through adoption or otherwise. I know I'm happy, though. Just as I once told my brother as we looked down at his sleeping daughter, I think I'm the luckiest guy in the world.

If you would like a more comprehensive explanation on how to put together an adoptive profile, check out Russell's book:

Hoping to Adopt:
How to Create the Ideal Adoption Profile

Here is how our letter read:

We can't begin to tell you how much love and respect we have for everybody who makes the difficult decision to place a child for adoption. We have been unable to have our own children, so we're incredibly grateful and excited about the prospect of adoption. Thank you for taking a moment to get to know us a little bit by reading our letter to you.

About Us

Our story began on a Sunday morning in church. With a little over a year left in college, Russell had just moved into a new apartment. Jammie had just moved to town a few days earlier and was staying with her parents while she looked for her own place. The timing couldn't have been any better. If Russell had moved to his new apartment a few weeks later, Jammie would have already been living in her place fifteen miles away. If Jammie had moved to the area a few weeks earlier, Russell wouldn't have spent that first Sunday with his eyes glued to the beautiful blonde across the room. It didn't take Russell very long to have her cornered as he introduced himself and found out her name. All of the usual steps of dating and going home to meet each other's families soon followed, and before long Russell was nervously standing in front of Jammie's father asking for his blessing to marry his daughter.

Jammie was born in Utah. She grew up being the only girl and the youngest sibling in the house until, when Jammie was 11 years old, her younger sister was born. Jammie would spend part of the day roughhousing with her three older brothers and then the rest of the day playing on the floor with her baby sister. She doesn't wrestle with her brothers anymore, and her baby sister is now a teenager, but it's still just as enjoyable to get together as a family.

Russell was born in Maryland and grew up as the fourth child out of six. While the Navy had Russell's family moving around a lot, he spent the majority of his younger years living in Nevada. He loved catching lizards and playing football or baseball with his siblings and friends out in the desert sand. All of Russell's siblings have moved out of Nevada, but everyone is still within driving distance and enjoys getting together as often as possible.

While growing up, Jammie's family watched rodeos and rode horses while Russell's family preferred watching baseball and tossing the ball around. Jammie's dad built saddles and programmed computers, while Russell's dad was a hospital administrator for the Navy. Jammie lived in the same house until she was 17 years old, while Russell lived in 10 different houses before he left for college at age 17. Jammie's house was mostly decorated with a country style, while Russell's house was mostly decorated with paintings and stained glass art done by family members. With all of the differences in styles, though, the similarities are much stronger. Both families love to keep in close contact. Both families love to get together whenever possible to ride horses or play softball. Both families would do anything for each other, and both families love each other more than anything.

How We Live

Russell graduated from college with a bachelor's degree in sociology and also graduated from a technical school with a degree as a dental laboratory technician. He worked for a few years under someone else before he and Jammie started their own dental lab business. At work in the dental lab, Russell does the majority of the work required to make gold and porcelain crowns, veneers, bridges, etc. Jammie stays at home to take care of our son, Ira. She helps Russell with the lab by taking charge of the finances, which she is able to do from home.

After graduating from college and moving to Boise, we spent the first few months searching for our perfect home. We weren't allowed any pets when we were living in our college apartment, so we were almost as excited to be able to get a dog as we were about getting our own house. On the first day we could move into our new house, we unloaded one truckload of our belongings and then went to pick out a dog, even before we went to get the second truckload of stuff. We now have two dogs, Bogey and Mulligan, and we chose them because their breeds are great as family dogs. Most of our friends have children, and our nieces and nephews are over all the time, so both dogs are great with kids.

Our Interests

We're never short of pictures from any event. Jammie loves photography and takes her nice camera just about everywhere she goes.

She mostly photographs weddings or family portraits, but she's done photo shoots with just about anyone or anything, and they all turn out beautifully. The only problem with her photography is that Russell often forgets to take the camera out of her hands, so she's not in as many pictures as he is.

When Russell was a teenager he never skipped a day of practicing his guitar. On most days, he'd come home late from working at the grocery store with his body being tired but his mind telling him otherwise. He would tell himself he'd just play for five minutes or so, but he always ended up strumming his six-string well past bedtime. The many hours of practice paid off. Russell has a band with two of his brothers who play with him on stage all around the Boise area. They are currently working on recording their fifth album.

Russell and Jammie both love to be active with all kinds of sports. Russell played baseball for his high school baseball team, so when he married Jammie, she took up the sport and has played on softball teams with him. Jammie played on her high school basketball team, so when she married Russell, he took up the sport too. Russell discovered disc golf (Frisbee golf) a few years before meeting Jammie, so she took up the sport and both have won many tournaments all around Idaho and Utah. Jammie discovered volleyball a few years before meeting Russell, so he took up that sport as well, and they have fun playing together on city league teams or just with other friends. Whatever sport it is, Russell and Jammie have probably tried it and enjoyed it.

No matter what our interest is, we enjoy doing it together. Jammie often comes up on stage to sing a song or two with Russell while he's performing. Russell goes with Jammie from time to time to *help her out with a photo shoot. Simply spending time together is the most important part. Russell and Jammie are best friends.*

With all of our interests, family has always been number one. Adoption has given us the gift of parenthood, which will always be at the top of our priority list.

Thank You

We can't fully understand everything you're going through, but we want you to know that we respect and love you very much. When that happy day does come and we're able to adopt again, we look forward to having an open and loving relationship with our child's birth parents, similar to the beautiful relationship we have with our son's birth family. We're excited to share updates as well as pictures, building our open relationship as we go. Again, thank you so much for taking the time to get to know us. If you'd like to see the current updates on our blog, or if you'd like to contact us, you can find us at:

xxxxxxx.blogspot.com

xxxxxxx@gmail.com

Open Adoption, Open Heart
on Facebook

Join us, where we discuss adoption topics, support one another, and find friends in the adoption community.

Other places to find Russell:

RussellElkins.com
Adoption.com
AdoptionBlogs.com
AdoptionVoicesMagazine.com

Hoping to Adopt: How to Create the Ideal Adoption Profile

It's hard to know how to choose the right photos for your profile and write the profile letter to potential birthparents. *Hoping to Adopt* is an excellent guide to tackling the task.

10 Adoption Essentials: What You Need to Know About Open Adoption

Adoption can be complicated and every situation is different, but *10 Adoption Essentials* helps simplify things by boiling it all down to ten things you need to know.

About the Author

Russell has always been a family man at heart. He and Jammie have adopted two beautiful children, Ira and Hazel, and have embraced their role as parents through open adoption. Both are actively engaged in the adoption community by communicating through social media, taking part in discussion panels, and writing songs about adoption.

Russell was born on Andrews Air Force Base near Washington, D.C. Along with his five siblings, he and his military family moved around a lot, living in eight different houses by the time he left for college at age 17. Although his family moved away from Fallon, Nevada, just a few months after he moved out, he still considers that little oasis in the desert to be his childhood hometown.

Even after leaving home, Russell always stayed close to his family. He shared an apartment with each of his three brothers at different times during his college career. They formed a band together back in the 1990s and still perform on a regular basis under the name of The Invisible Swordsmen.

After nearly a decade of college and changing his major a few times, Russell received his bachelor's degree in sociology from Brigham Young University in Provo, Utah. He later graduated from Ameritech College where he learned the trade of being a dental lab technician. Along with writing both fiction and non-fiction, Russell owns and operates Elkins Dental Lab located in Meridian, Idaho.

12243604R00062

Printed in Great Britain
by Amazon.co.uk, Ltd.,
Marston Gate.